AF226122

Colours of the Alphabet

Volume 2

By Sarah McPherson

Colours of the Alphabet – Volume 2

Written by Sarah McPherson

First Printing, 2022

Published by Tarva Publishing
www.tarvapublishing.com.au

ISBN 978-0-6454104-8-8

To Katie

Thanks for introducing me to more colours

There are many colours of the
Alphabet
in that we do agree,

From Almond, Amazon and Amber
to colours like Zaffre

So can you see your favorite
with the A–Z of colour

Or if you had made this book
would you choose another?

A

Acid Green

B

Blue

C

cyan

D

Dark Orange

E

Eggplant

F

Flame

G

Gold (Metallic)

H

Helioptrope

I

Imperial Red

J

Jade

K

Komby Green

L

Lilac

M

Mango

N

Nickel

Orchid

P

Pear

Q

Queen Blue

R

Rose

S

Saffron

Teal

U

unmellow Yellow

Volt

W

wisteria

xanthic

Y

Yale Blue

Z

zaffre

So did you see your favorite,
colour in our book?

Head back to the start and
take another look!

Red, orange, yellow, green, blue, purple, pink, grey, brown, black, indigo, violet,